MW01205436

Working and Writing for Change
Edited by Steve Parks and Jess Pauszek

WORKING AND WRITING FOR CHANGE
Series Editors: Steve Parks & Jess Pauszek

The Working and Writing for Change series began during the 100th anniversary celebrations of NCTE. It was designed to recognize the collective work of teachers of English, Writing, Composition, and Rhetoric to work within and across diverse identities to ensure the field recognize and respect language, educational, political, and social rights of all students, teachers, and community members. While initially solely focused on the work of NCTE/CCCC Special Interest Groups and Caucuses, the series now includes texts written by individuals in partnership with other communities struggling for social recognition and justice.

Books in the Series
CCCC/NCTE Caucuses
History of the Black Caucus National Council Teachers of English by Marianna White Davis
Listening to Our Elders: Working and Writing for Social Change by Samantha Blackmon, Cristina Kirklighter, and Steve Parks
Building a Community, Having a Home: A History of the Conference on College Composition and Communication edited by Jennifer Sano-Franchini, Terese Guinsatao Monberg, K. Hyoejin Yoon
Dreams and Nightmares: I Fled Alone to the United States When I Was Fourteen by Liliana Velázquez. Edited and translated by Mark Lyons

Community Publications
Pro(se)letariets: The Writing of the Trans-Atlantic Worker Writer Federation, edited by Audrey Burns, Alicia Landsberg, Evan Smith, Jesse Uruchima
PHD to PhD: How Education Saved My Life by Elaine Richardson
The Weight of My Armor: Creative Nonfiction and Poetry by the Syracuse Veterans' Writing Group

PRO(SE)LETARIETS

The Writing of the Trans-Atlantic
Worker Writer Federation

Edited by
Audrey Burns
Alicia Landsberg
Evan Smith
Jesse Uruchima

Parlor Press
Anderson, South Carolina
www.parlorpress.com

Parlor Press LLC, Anderson, South Carolina, USA
© 2010 New City Community Press
Printed in the United States of America on acid-free paper.

S A N: 2 5 4 - 8 8 7 9

Library of Congress Cataloging-in-Publication Data on File

2 3 4 5

978-1-60235-954-3 (paperback)
978-1-60235-959-8 (PDF)

Working and Writing for Change Series
Edited by Steve Parks

Cover photograph by Margaret Swift
Cover title by Sadie Shorr-Parks
Interior design by Elizabeth Parks, elizabethannparks@gmail.com

Parlor Press, LLC is an independent publisher of scholarly and trade titles in print and multimedia formats. This book is available in paper, cloth and eBook formats from Parlor Press on the World Wide Web at http://www.parlorpress.com or through online and brick-and-mortar bookstores. For submission information or to find out about Parlor Press publications, write to Parlor Press, 3015 Brackenberry Drive, Anderson, South Carolina, 29621, or email editor@parlorpress.com.

CONTENTS

PRO(SE)LETARIETS

Preface

Steve Parks, Syracuse University
Nick Pollard, Sheffield Hallam University
Federation of Worker Writers and Community Publishers

Six years ago, in a Syracuse University classroom, three students quietly talked about the lack of working class voices in their classrooms. There was working class "literature" to be sure. But working class voices, actual working class students, seemed rare. In such an environment, they wondered how their experiences of labor, of motherhood, of being working class, could be recognized, validated, or legitimated by the wealthy students around them.

The Trans-Atlantic Worker Writer Federation grew from this moment of alienation. As educators, separated by the Atlantic ocean, but sharing a commitment to working class students, we decided this moment could not be repeated. Working together, we developed a series of courses at Syracuse University focused on working class writing. Each course was linked to a local Syracuse union writing group, the Basement Writers, as well as to the Federation of Worker Writers and Community Publishers (FWWCP), a national network of similar groups in the United Kingdom that had existed for over 30 years. (To learn more about the FWWCP, see *The Republic of Letters: Working Class Writing and Local Publishing*.)

Working together, students, local writers, FWWCP members shared their experiences and ideas on how a working class background shaped their education. Through phone conversations, blogs, on-line writing prompts, group meetings and trans-Atlantic travel, Syracuse University students studied the rich history of the FWWCP, wrote new pieces in response, and, then, revised in the context of a writing community that bridged the Atlantic. Collectively, these writings tell the progress of a working-student, through the early years of education, the difficult pathway through university or trade school, the entry into the world of work, and the political sensibility that is created by these experiences.

This anthology represents only a portion of that writing from the past and present that shaped this project. Indeed, we hope this publication shows the conversation made possible by a rich tradition and new insights. In the following pages, you will see how a piece of FWWCP writing from 25 years ago resonates with the writing of a current Syracuse University student; how the struggles of working students in the USA today intersect with those of working mothers in the UK; how students across generations and oceans have consistently fought off attempts to denigrate their heritage, learning to speak out about the values that sustain both them and their communities.

The following pages, then, represent a conversation among writers, among working class communities, and among different citizens about the common struggles facing the working class student. Most importantly, more than recording the struggle, these pieces record the ability of the working class to succeed as writers and as working class activists.

Introduction

Alicia Landsberg and Audrey Burns

Literature is valued because it captures the variety and depth of the human experience, but does literature value all writers? Capture all experiences? Should producing great literature require a mastery of language, something that only those properly "trained" can take part in? Or can working class people, from all walks of the world, use the written word to effectively express their experience of the world? *Proseletariets* is premised on the belief not only that working class writers can, but they do. To truly understand this point, however, we as readers must expand and reform what is defined as "literature" and who are respected as "writers." We must learn to read and understand writing differently.

Proseletariets provides this opportunity. This book showcases literature by writers that may have not had access to extensive literary schooling, who may not choose to write in a style and voice that is traditionally recognized as valuable to literature. Yet we ask you to understand these pieces as giving voice to the "human experiences" that cross over the Atlantic, from working class communities in the United Kingdom to the United States, as displaying literary merit, and debunking the unspoken belief that a proper "writer" must have a Ph.D and long list of publications attached to their name.

Many of the writers in this book are members of the UK-based Federation of Working Writers and Community

Publishers (FWWCP). They are men and women of all ages and varying backgrounds. But they all have one thing in common; they have a story to tell. For the past five years, they joined their stories with students and workers in Syracuse, New York, to explore what collectively they might have in common. As you will read, the common experiences of being working class in "classrooms" soon became a primary topic. Through their writing, they asked: What type of education do the working class receive? What is really being taught? How do those lessons affect the rest of their life? How does education need to be reformed?

To organize their insights and ideas, this book is organized into four sections. We begin with "Early Days," a section that chronicles the early educational experiences of working class writers, charting the forces that would place them as "outsiders" in years to come. The second section, "Holding On," details challenges faced by the working class as they move onto higher education and early adulthood- whether it is in the academic or work environment that poses the challenge. In "Working Days," the third section, the writers go on to illustrate the hardships faced by working class writers in their later lives as employees, parents, and citizens. Between these sections, there are "Inserts" where the personal and political experiences of those involved in this collaborative writing project are explored. The publication concludes, in section four, "Future Actions," with the "Transfed Manifesto," a manifesto developed by writers in this project to express their collective sense of what an education would look like that helps us recognize and appreciate what makes us unique and binds us as humans.

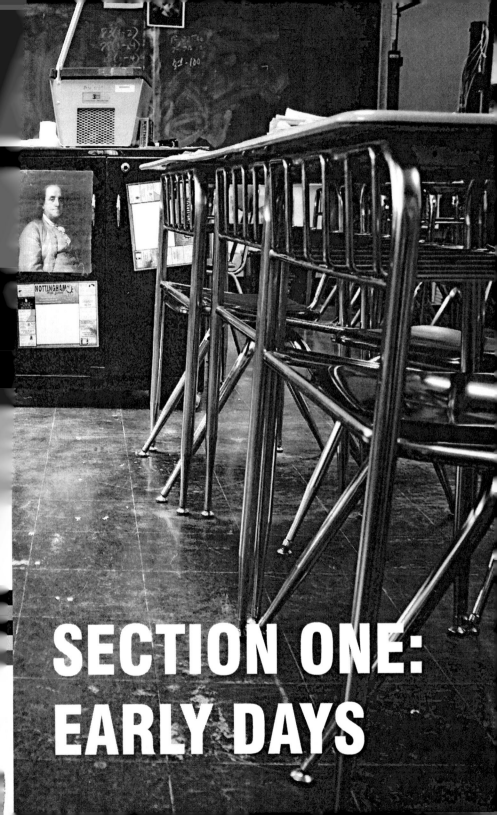

SECTION ONE:
EARLY DAYS

Deana Cater, The First Day of Third Grade (USA)

When I was younger, say around six or seven, I was a little fireball. I learned all of my lessons, but I learned them better than any of the other second graders. I was brilliant, passionate, confident and not afraid to speak out. I could wow all of my teachers and peers and without even noticing or trying. We had these little journals we were supposed to write in everyday. Every morning before we began our lessons, we would take 15 minutes or so to write in them. They'd be simple prompts like "What do you want to be when you grow up?" or "What did you do this weekend?", and because I learned my lessons so well, I didn't need to think about it. I'd get all fired up about the prompt and put pen to paper and begin scribbling. It was like the lessons were innate. I was born to write and to write well. I was never sure exactly how I was writing that made my teachers smile and point and brag to other teachers about what a brilliant little fireball I was, intact, I didn't think I was doing anything out of the ordinary, but whatever I was doing, I kept it because it worked.

Soon after completing the second grade, my parents decided to send me to another school. They told me that I would be going to a school in a better area, a more influential part of town far away from the rinkydink part of town I knew. They told me that there were more opportunities where I was going. Better education, more money, and the people were the movers and shakers of the city. They were confident that I would fit right in. They knew their little fireball would just assimilate right into that culture. Everyone was so excited about the move. All of my family knew it was the best thing for me, and my teachers and peers cheered me on and supported the decision. They all thought that I could fare well in this new part of town. "Not too many of us over here get a chance to go over that way," my 60-year-old neighbor told me "and worse yet, not all of us do so well when we get over there, but you're a little fireball, you'll do fine."

Soon after the move was my first day of third grade. I wake up, excited to experience the great opportunity that everyone was telling me about. I wash extra good so I'm extra squeaky clean. I think I washed my face three times. I put on my best outfit. Have mom fix my hair just right in braided pigtails. My dad bought me a new Hello Kitty bookbag with a matching lunchbox. Oh yes hunny, I thought I was looking sharp, draped down and done up. I kiss my parents goodbye and they wished me well as I boarded the city school bus.

I watched the trees whip by the bus window. Even the trees are more beautiful in this new place. The grass is greener. The houses are bigger, better, brighter. There are cool looking cars riding alongside the bus. There were kids around my age sitting in the back seat of these cars, I suppose getting dropped off to school. Some of the cars names are easier to pronounce than others. "Hummer," I whisper to myself before looking at another vehicle behind it. "Fer ...feraer.. .feaer... , no, looks like a short 'a', ferar... ferari," I whisper wondering to myself.

Finally, I arrived at my new school. I walk through the heavy, glass double doors. Then I stand, looking. These people, these new people don't look like me. I walk around a little bit. No one looks like me. They wear their hair differently. They walk differently. Even dress differently. I begin to think that maybe I don't look as sharp as I thought. I've seen some of these people before. I've seen them pass through my old town from time to time. I've seen them on television, too, advertising their boat dealerships and restaurants. I've seen people that look like them on billboards. These look like the type of people that run for mayor or governor or justice chair or whatever else.

I walk up to a student to ask if she would show me around. We begin to converse, but I can hardly understand from the way she was speaking. She was speaking the same language, no doubt, but it was as if she was speaking a different dialect. I had to listen carefully to catch snippets of her phrases to piece together what she was saying to me. I was thinking to myself that maybe she's new to the country, but she introduces me to a lot of her friends and teachers and they were speaking in the same manner. So perhaps I do not speak correctly. Perhaps I need to try to speak like them I wonder to myself.

"Would my parents understand me?" I ask myself.

She continues to show me around the school and introduces me to another student who is in my class. The student looks puzzled. She speaks the same as all the rest of the people in the school, so it was hard to understand again, but I believe she asked me if I was dirty. "Dirty?" I asked, "why do you think I'm dirty?"

"When my little brother plays outside on our jungle gym, sometimes he gets brown dirt spots on him. You look like you have them all over. Did you wash this morning? Did you fall on your way to school?"

I try to explain to her that I'm not dirty, but she has a hard time understanding. I guess she's never seen anyone like me before. I begin to wonder where she must live that she has never had a friend of darker skin.

Finally, it's time for class. We all pile into our little desks. The teacher begins to write a series of sentences on the board as a student volunteer passes out spiral bound notebooks. I begin to get excited because I recognize this activity. It's journal time. The teacher explains we will write a series of quick writes of about two paragraphs each. We will stop after each prompt and select volunteers to share theirs before we begin the next one. We'll complete three prompts.

The first prompt was "What did you do this summer?". This is easy enough I think to myself. I let the words fall onto the paper. I begin to write about the trips to the park with my parents, going to the swimming pool, and visiting my grandparents. I write about how my grandparents make the best barbecue ribs and how I prefer my dad to make Koolaid because he puts more sugar in it than Mom does. I scribble, erase, and scribble until I am confident that I have the best two paragraphs possible.

The teacher asks for volunteers to share their writing. Immediately, my hand shoots up, but as luck would have it, she calls on someone else. A boy stands and begins to read. He tells us of his summer trip to Mazatlan, Mexico. Another student gets called on next and tells us of her sailing trip with her family in their boat along the east coast. Another student spent a few weeks at her family's beach house. My story doesn't sound so great anymore. Their experiences are all so different than mine. Would they even relate to my experiences? Would they care since theirs seem so much more worthwhile? The way they write even sounds different. Their word choice and the way they put things together doesn't quite sound like my style. "I bet they don't even drink Koolaid," I say to myself.

The time comes for the last prompt. "Who is your role model?" I decide to write about my grandmother, and her struggles raising nine brothers and sisters while her parents left to find work in another state. It was taking me a while to get started this time. Nothing was sounding right. Everyone else seems to not be having a problem. Am I the only one struggling? Everyone else seems to be comfortable and doing well. The ideas weren't coming as quickly, in fact, writing was becoming a chore. I wasn't sure if I should try to write like them again, or just go back to how I write. The problem is, I never had to think about it before. I'm not sure what to do, but I finally pound out something.

This time when the teacher asks for volunteers my hand stays down. Volunteer after volunteer stands up to read and I listen, wondering what it was about their writing that sounds different, asking myself if it's possible for me to write like they write, or if I should continue to not think about it and let it just come, like I've been doing.

Soon, school ends. I wave goodbye to many of the friends I made that day as their parents come one by one to pick them up. I board the city bus to go home. My parents ask me about my first day of school and I tell them with a smile that I had a great day and that I made a lot of friends.

Morning comes. It's the second day of third grade. I try to fake sick so that I wouldn't have to go, but my parents are too smart for that. I get out of bed. I go to my closet. Nothing looks right. I scramble about trying to put together a better outfit than before. I then wash extra, extra squeaky clean this time. I think I washed my face five times. There's no way anyone can say I'm, dirty now. I board the bus to school after kissing my parents goodbye. I look at the trees whip by thinking about what kind of prompts the teacher will assign today, asking myself if it will be as difficult today as it was yesterday and if I have what it takes to make it in this new school.

Lynne Clayton, Untitled (UK)

These ramblings are my own experiences, perceptions and reflections. They're not meant to be an official history; I don't know how to go about one of them. (For Real Historians: I think I am a Primary Source - or is this just another delusion!)

I was educated in Peckham, in the borough of Southwark, South East London, in the 50's and 60's. In those days, as now, Southwark was a very poor place, with Peckham having a bad reputation as a very rough (working class) area. I went to the local primary school, called Grove Vale, a redbrick Victorian building surrounded by tall iron railings with a narrow black tarmac rim in between which was our playground. The infant's school was on the ground floor and we all started there when we were five. After two years we went up to the primary school for another four years.

I was with the same bunch of kids in the same class all the way through. Boys and girls were taught together at that age, and in mixed ability groups, as they still are. (One major difference between then and now, of course, is that no immigrant kids joined us till I was ten.) We spent much of the last year practicing for our first public exam, the Eleven Plus (11+), which was designed to test our "intelligence". This was a very important exam, as it determined what kind of education we would get in the future.

It was also a very difficult exam to pass; only 25% of us got through. Passing meant going to the local grammar school, modeled to some extent on public schools, with a strong "academic" tradition of study and the promise of some sort of "respectable" middle class career. At the end of five years, aged 16, we took our next set of public exams, called 0 levels. ("0" stands for Ordinary). If we got high enough grades, and our parents could afford it, we went on to do A levels in the 6th form. If we got high enough grades for these, then we could go to college or university (some of us even got a grant in those heady days) and the world was our oyster.

In fact, it was even more difficult to pass the 11+ if you were a girl; the Government hadn't expected that girls would perform so well (better than the boys, as it happens!), and they hadn't provided enough grammar school places – so they upped the pass mark for girls – honestly. Interestingly, fifty years later, girls still outperform boys in exams, only now it's more openly acknowledged.

On the other hand, failing the 11+ meant going to the local Secondary Modern school where the emphasis was much more on practical, manual skills, and the only exam on offer, if at all, was the Certificate of Secondary Education (CSE). In other words, passing the 11+ in Peckham was an invitation to join the middle classes! I have often wondered, in my paranoid state of mind, if it was all a deliberate Government ploy to harvest the "clever" working class kids and instill them with middle class culture so that they became a part of the bourgeoisie and didn't want to foment a revolution anymore.

The word was out; give the working classes more genuine opportunities, aren't we a wonderful Government, vote for us, etc. Yes, for me it was without doubt an empowering experience. The grammar school I went to, called Honor Oak, at one end of Peckham Rye, was for girls only. It was a very pleasant building, an open square with the classrooms overlooking the well-kept inner lawn, and its own extensive grounds including a huge front lawn, separated from the hockey pitch by a small stream, as well as tennis courts and a rose garden (for sixth formers only). There was also a small music block and a three storey science block was added while I was there. I describe these lovely facilities because I want to contrast them with the school my sister went to - unlike me, she failed the 11+. Her school was an old Victorian building with some tarmac round it. Oh, and they had a bike shed.

Whatever the reasoning behind it, the grammar school scheme meant lots more working class kids getting into higher education, including me. And when I emerged, bright-eyed and bushy-tailed at the age of 22, I had accumulated more numbers and letters than I knew what to do with.

Was I duped? Oh yes, I swallowed it hook, line and sinker. When I got my first teaching job in Peckham, I was determined to give back all I had gained. I suppose I must have felt a bit like the Pied Piper; I would lead them on an educational journey that would free them from the entrapments of poverty.

Luckily it didn't take me long to stop being a pawn of the Government and become a traitor, a subversive teacher instead. (All it took was my first lesson, in a "sink" secondary modern girls' school. My Head of Department had kindly given me a "bright" class of 14 year olds just about to begin their CSE studies, and I thought that such girls would love the romantic story of "Jane Eyre", just as I had done. It was on the exam syllabus, so what could go wrong? Nothing, except that none of them could read it). But that's another story.

Bruce Barnes, Untitled (UK)

"It's bedsits', what else would you expect", his puzzled expression said, having opened the door to us, on a street in North West London: Mr. B's study, the classroom for declining Latin verbs, the first floor toilets for water-bombing and getting caned for it, were part of the house's history that he never knew. Private education in the UK can be quite private, even the terminology of schooling is elusive; there are private schools that act as feeder schools for public schools, which are private fee paying secondary schools too. (Schools supported by public funds are referred to as being part of the state education system.)

From 11 to 14, what was "W.H." school educated me in the foibles and idiosyncrasies of life, and I'm grateful to my teachers, now resting in the staffroom upstairs, for lessons that have stuck far better than the regular curriculum: help those who need a break (as the headmaster, Mr. B, did by recruiting teachers that mainstream schools rejected), listen quietly to someone's pain, (as we did with our English master, tackling bouts of depression), enjoy chaos when it happens, (the running fights between the art teacher and the school cook), never inflict pain unless you are skilled at it, (Mr. A, the Latin master, also worked as a wrestler), dishonesty benefits the individual in the short term, (teachers helped me with my exam paper for public school), but stores up bad karma (the school closed after a tabloid newspaper exposé).

My father was a German Jew, who came to Britain as a refugee at the beginning of the Second World War, and was temporarily deported to Australia as an "enemy alien". On his return to Britain, he married my mother, an Anglican from East Anglia, from a working class background. I feel privileged to have my education, but I don't think my parents were fully aware of what it entailed. Private education is often seen as privileged, but small classes, personal attention, and a stimulating curriculum should be freely available to all.

Pat Smart, Untitled (UK)

This is where I make a twit of myself! I've always considered myself totally non-political ... no that's not right, what I really mean is I don't understand a bleeping thing about it! But here we go... I lived in Public Housing but we termed it differently, to us it was Council Housing, as the words Public Housing to me, and probably my family also, meant for posh people, those even posher than people who were buying their own houses. In our area there were neighbours on our row of terraced houses who were buying, they, to me, were people who had better jobs than me Dad, but, people who were rich enough to send their kids to Public School were, to me, like royalty, really rich! So the word Public to me at that time, wasn't sort of linked to (as I know) the general public or people, it was a word used by and for posh people (I know, how sad can you get!).

I went to a Roman Catholic school, which was all divided up, boys couldn't go to the same schools as girls, I used to find that strange, you could play with boys in your street, but mustn't mix with them in school! But at the same time, our girl's school was too small, or there were far more girls than boys, whatever, so we had to borrow some classrooms on the boys side of the road, we had to use their playground too (at different times though) and were made to play netball with our pleated school uniform skirts tucked inside our knickers, okay if you had on the "posh" navy-blue (costly - to my family) ones. I often had to go to school in me Mam's flowery ones with a pin to keep them up, but I was still made to tuck me (not quite the correct uniform pleated skirt) into them. The boys could crowd into the corridors of the top floor to have a good "blimp" (oggle) at the girls, often with the male teachers getting a blimp behind them also. What I'm trying to say is, even in the state-run (Catholic-run) schools there were class divides also. I know I was one of the poorest ones, so I was the scruff, the "thicko", the stupid one whose parents couldn't afford the correct school uniform, I was poor, so, therefore I was stupid, etc..., etc... (even the school's head mistress, a nun, told me so quite often usually when she was giving me "six of the best" (a good whacking with a long cane on each of my hands).

There are more issues in the above about how I grew up, (by no fault of my parents, if they had the money when times weren't so lean, they would spend a lot on better food and better, still second-hand but posher, second-hand clothing), as well as in my education. There were plenty of kids who went to the same school as me who went on to college and a few to university, but they all came from the homes with parents in better jobs. You may think, what's that got to do with it? Well I can only say what I believe, because I was one of the "scruffs" I was pushed aside, left at the back, not included in discussions etc in class. If I put my hand up to ask a question one certain teacher would give me a "withering" look and tell me to put my hand down. When I did get to ask a question I was usually told, "because I said so!" or "don't be stupid girl!" I wasn't the only one; there were quite a few of us. So that kind of thing (class divide – no pun intended!) certainly did "impinge" on my education.

Jo Barnes, Scholarship Boy (UK)

He knocked at the door.

"Come in sit down.

Now what newspapers do your parents read?"

"The Pictorial and the Daily Herald, sir."

"Who is your favourite comedian, boy?"

"Max Miller, sir!!"

"Tell us one of his jokes."

"I can't remember one, but I can tell you one of Frankie Howard's."

"What does your father do?"

"He's a docker, sir."

Each word a nail hammered his fate.

Their words, his words.

Not grammar school material, they said.

Lyndi Halpern, Untitled (USA)

I remember stepping on the train like it was yesterday. I waited on the platform. 7:14AM. I was nervous, anxious, excited, shaking. I was lucky enough to be accompanied by my mother. My mother with coffee and cell phone in hand. With me, but not. There to tell me everything would be ok, but so unconvincing with her earpiece jammed into her ear, speaking in a gibberish tongue about grants and funding. After our 20 minute ride on the Long Island Rail Road, we arrive at Woodside, and once again I'm told to wait. Wait, like it was that easy. While on the platform I noticed various groups of friends, playing around, joking. A black boy with his toes over the edge, balancing mischievously as a nearby sign warns passengers to stay behind the yellow line.

A group of Spanish girls speaking as though they were characters on La Novella, talking a mile a minute, me with my elementary knowledge of the language listening on but barely comprehending. Dios Mio! Another group of boys, casually talking about their decision to attend a performing arts school. Most of them cute. Me, the little girl clutching to her mom. Note to self: they know you're scared.

My mom opens her mouth and begins talking about needing a vacation as she comments on how unusually cold is it, pulling at her Burberry jacket for added warmth. I notice eyes staring, robbing me of any confidence I had. Post script on note to self: leave mom at home. We board the shaky 7 train and after five stops arrive at 33rd Street. I'm relieved to exit considering the awkward train ride. Friends talking, laughing; my mom unable to maintain any sort of balance, nearly killing one of the cute boys. Typical. The part of me dying to fit in wants to tell her to go home.

That I can walk to 29th Street on my own. Even still, the overwhelmingly scared part of me urges her to walk with me. We walk in silence. I am dying to hold her hand, but I refrain. I am shocked and thrown off by my feelings of loneliness and my seemingly relentless inability to feel comfortable.

Suddenly my new jeans aren't so important. I would die to actually feel as comfortable as the denim that conforms to my body. I futz around with the diamond ring I received as a Bat Mitzvah gift and notice it has become loose from sweat. We approach the doors of the building. There are crowds, clicks, handshakes, high fives. I'm anxious. Bye Mom. Post post script on note to self: hugs with your mother in public should not exceed two minutes. Awkward.

Friends who knew each other in ages past hug, while others smile as they meet for the first time. Teachers anxiously attempt to quiet down the massive swarm of barely post pubescent adolescents, but the roar of the crowd is too loud, the excitement too overwhelming, a hundred 14-16 year old students hyped off coffee and Red Bull, and me, with my mother. My mother who usually provides me with such comfort, such warmth, suddenly made me feel more cold and empty than I had ever felt before. I felt so young, so inconsolably alone. Like I should have hopped on the train by myself that morning, should have done this on my own like every other kid. I was beating myself up for having a mother who would do anything for me, and it took me until now to realize this.

When she finally left we departed by studio. Drama one way, dance another, fine arts, instrumental, vocal. We took the elevator in groups up to the fourth floor. Opening up earlier than expected, Frank Sinatra School of the Arts in its first year was given a sale hallway in LaGuardia Community College in Long Island City, NY, an industrial mecca located just minutes outside of Manhattan. It was a change from Bayside where I had attended school my whole life. Northeast Queens generally populated by upper-middle class Jewish families, heavily endowed by arts organizations and extremely high graduation rates. Upon first glance, Long Island City was dirty and cold. It was a change, a scary one, but one I was ready to embark on. Sans mother.

Packed into the elevator like pimentos into Spanish olives, I was overwhelmed by the diversity I witnessed. It was like the cover of a textbook or something. Black, White, Hispanic, Asian, Native American, in wheelchairs, on crutches, with long hair, with no hair. Both ends of the spectrum and everywhere in between were represented in this tiny hallway of this tiny school.

When we finally got upstairs, we were put into classrooms according to major. We were briefly spoken to about what was expected of us, given papers to fill out, and then did introductions. Our first drama instructor was a black woman, as poised as Oprah, with a bigger, presence than God. She talked about her struggles to get where she was today, as she pushed her bangs out of her eyes, making a stack of beautiful gold bangles visible. She talked about her upbringing in the Bronx, her love for her drama and her son whom she was single handedly raising. She spoke about how her biggest expectation of us was that we put one hundred and ten percent into every assignment we were given, and that we work together with people we might never befriend outside of the classroom. We then went around as students and introduced ourselves. This was not the Jewish geography I was used to from sleepaway camp. No Jamie from Long Island or Alyson from North New Jersey. Instead it was LaShonda, a tall, confident black girl from Brooklyn. Ryan, a small, white, Irish boy from Maspeth, Queens. One of the few boys in the drama major. Kay, a short Filipino girl with cut up clothing and bangs that covered her entire forehead. Me...Lyndi from Bayside, whose mom brought her to school.

I was nervous, shaking, anxious, similar to how I felt while waiting on the platform. Just like the train that I knew was going to come, I knew that I would soon fit in, that my "train would come" and I would not board lonely and afraid, clutching to my mother. I knew that soon I'd be waiting on the platform prepared, ready, eager. That I would board with friends, familiar faces, and eventually know beforehand who I'd sit with. But I didn't know when that time would come and the uncertainty killed me.

That first year at Frank Sinatra School of the Arts I grew more as a person than I think at any other time in my life. There were days when I felt nervous, shaking, and anxious, but there even more days when I felt calm. When I felt ready. I met an exuberant amount of people, and learned so much from them that I was eventually able to apply to myself. I discovered in me qualities I never knew I possessed, and developed skills and talents that I truly believe I would not have been able to do anywhere else. It was during my second year however, as a sophomore, that I really became culturally aware and appreciated diversity more than ever before. We had a new drama instructor hailing from Milwaukee, Wisconsin, who had the idea to write a play, as a class, and workshop it, performing it for students and staff and ultimately organizations whose goals

revolved around making the world a more culturally safe and aware place.

After much deliberation, it was decided that the piece was to be called "The Names That Hurt" and featured vulgar and controversial terms such as "Nigger," "sore," "Kike," and "Wop." The piece also shed light on eating disorders and derogatory terms based around body image but the primary goal of the piece was to educate based on race.

Some pieces took a comedic role, while others brought audience members to tears. More than the final per-formance however, the writing of these monologues and scenes was the most rewarding part. Partnering with peers whom I might have never associated with, hearing their stories of being put down and called nasty terms, was extremely beneficial to me not only as a student and an actor, but as a person.

The play was an enormous success. Planned only to do an afternoon and an evening performance, we extended the dates and eventually performed it at St. John's University at a conference and passed our scripts down to underclassmen that still perform it four years later.

Writing the play, performing the play, taught me so much. I wouldn't consider myself sheltered, but this experience was innumerably beneficial. I also feel that I have passed on what I learned, not necessarily in a direct way, other than performing the piece and verbally educating. It would be utopian and unrealistic to think that I sat with my family like the Brady's or the Seaver's, while violins play softly in the background, enhancing the intensity as we discuss the stigma of derogatory terms and how it has affected our lives. Even though my passing on of knowledge may not have been direct, I think I've handled myself differently and better in certain situations, been more aware of the comments I make and the stereotypes I used to automatically accept as true. I think in general my behavior has changed because of increased awareness and I am forever grateful.

As stated earlier, I was a nervous wreck entering this new world when I came to high school. I had been scared enough as I watched Full House and other 90s sitcoms that depicted high school as the utmost scary place to enter alone. Filled with cheerleaders who would eat you and jocks who would give you wedgies. These situations haunted my dreams that became nightmares as high school became nearer and nearer, however when the decision to attend FSSA was made, my fears transformed entirely. I was no longer worried about the blonde girl with pom poms making fun of me. Now I had to worry about Spanish girls hitting me with their violins, gay boys making fun of me for being spoiled. It was a whole new world, and I can't say I was ready.

Embarking upon the journey of entering FSSA in Long Island City was a risk I'm happy I took. I graduated with three best best friends whom I can't say are completely out of my realm of "normality" in terms of friends I've had my whole life, people that I needed to go to Frank Sinatra to meet, however it's where I met them, and though they ultimately could have been friends I might have made at sleepaway camp or back in Bayside, Long Island City is where our friendship began and where it blossomed. Though they might not be my best friends I also became lifelong companions with people of every race and ethnicity, every financial background. I had friends I could meet in Manhattan and go to dinner and a show with, and friends I could go to McDonalds after school with. Friends whose parents became friends with mine, and friends who had no parents.

Though there were times when class division was apparent, such as when it came time to pay for costumes and chip in money for class trips, my high school created an environment where this line that seemingly divided the classes was blurred and everyone was welcome.

It is now my sophomore year in college, a mere yet an entire four years since "The Names That Hurt", a whole five years since I entered Frank Sinatra School of the Arts. I have grown enormously, however I still feel a feeling of guilt that pains me from time to time. A feeling of guilt that pains me when I have too much time on my hands and I'm sitting and thinking. A feeling of guilt that pains me day in and day out, and is something I cannot get rid of. I cannot change what I was born into or where I stand, and this feeling of being stuck in between a rock and a hard place, the pressure of a boulder making my appreciation for privilege turn into angst, tears at my insides and pulls on my heart, making me yearn to change. I am immeasurably thankful for all I have, yet it seems to me that privilege is like a double edged sword. It allows for you to get so much, but upon retrieval of whatever it is you are getting, privilege strikes at you, puncturing you with guilt. Sometimes the pain is immediate, and sometimes it takes an assignment to make this realization and for the pain to hit, but regardless, it hits, and it hits hard. Coming to college last year you can bet I had my mom right by my side. And this time I was even brave enough to hold her hand.

Virginie Pithon, Untitled (UK)

For as long as anyone can remember (or at least, for as long as I can remember, which admittedly isn't very long in the grand scheme of things) there has always been great debate on what education ought to be like and how it ought to be carried out. Do we need to be harsher? Or more encouraging? Offer a broader range of subjects? Fewer, more specialized subjects? How exactly do we go about preparing the (god help us) "future leaders of the world"?

Well, I for one can only speak for myself. How would I describe the perfect education system? To be honest, I don't even know where to begin. The perfect education system should challenge its students, urge them to work hard but not so hard that they don't have the time to experience that very important little thing called life. It should encourage students to work to their full potential and to aim high – regardless of abilities. The worst thing a teacher can say to a student is "No you can't." And any teacher who does so has definitely failed on some level, at least as far as I'm concerned. But at the same time teachers should be realistic. Most students can see through empty comments of encouragement, and they will not thank you for it. Be honest with regards to a students' abilities and potential – but don't ever shut them down and tell them that they can't do something or that they shouldn't even bother trying. That the perfect education system should be "a safe environment free from traditional social/economic biases with self-respect for each other as individuals as well as members of different classes, heritages and sexualities" goes without saying. It is terribly sad that in the twenty-first century something as fundamental as equality and respect for one another still needs to be reiterated. But even though all these things are true, or what I believe to be true, for me education needs to go further than that still.

Perhaps it's the remnants of the young teenage-idealist in me. But I wish that education (and knowledge more generally) were seen as something valuable in and of itself, rather than a means to an end: getting a job. Now don't get me wrong, I'm not saying that education shouldn't be practical and job-skills driven. I just don't see why the two seem to be more and more seen as mutually exclusive. Too often you hear students complaining about how what they learn will never serve them in the real world. Why do we waste our time learning all these things we'll never ever use again once we leave academia? What is the point? Why bother? In an educational system that has truly done its job, such questions would be absurd.

In a perfect education system, knowledge would be seen as something valuable in its own right – regardless of whether it's useful or not (in my personal belief there is no such thing as "useless" knowledge, but humour me for a moment here). Moreover, education should aim to instill a love and curiosity for knowledge in all its students. Ok, so not every teacher can be like Robin Williams in Dead Poets Society – nor would I or anyone else expect them to be. But my biggest fear with regards to education is how too often, the process of merely jumping through hoops and force-feeding information without giving knowledge itself any importance, can create a generation of students who feel entirely apathetic and detached from this thing called education; students who are merely going through the motions so that they can all eventually move on to "Real Life," whatever that may be.

Furthermore, education shouldn't just concern itself with

teaching us facts and theories. It should also concern itself with creating discerning individuals capable of thinking critically and questioning the information that they are given. Now I know that this is already the goal of most schools and universities – that perhaps I am preaching to the converted here. But if I say it, it's because there are still too many people who take things at face-value and don't bother to look beneath the surface, to investigate the other side of the argument or to try and understand a different point of view. All these things we do in class aren't just confined to essays and dissertations – they are real essential skills that need to be applied in real life, everyday. How can we effectively arm ourselves against misinformation and ignorance if critical thinking and analysis is seen as something that is done only in the classroom?

These two issues, I think, work together. A natural curiosity and yearning to understand more drives people to read beyond the surface of things, to have a better comprehension of the world around them. And it is only when we have a better understanding of the world and all the other individuals in it that we can realistically expect all education to be "a safe environment free from traditional social/economic biases with self-respect for each."

THE VALUE OF EDUCATION
YOU DECIDE WHAT YOU'RE WORTH
Average monthly earnings
without a high school diploma:
$450
Average monthly earnings
with a high school diploma:
$921
Mathematics
Average monthly earnings with
a college degree
$1,829
Average monthly earnings
with a doctorate degree
$3,637

THE TRANSFED WRITER

Ann Marie Taliercio (USA) by Sharon Clott

Ann Marie Taliercio believes in spirits.

She believes in psychics, the modern-day oracles, to capture the essence of spirits. She believes that spirits breathe life. She believes in the spirit of humans, cats, dogs, animals, and even spirits in little bugs. She believes every piece of wood, pencils and paper contain a spirit, just as trees and nature do as well. She is a spiritual person in all of her ways: the way she lives, the way she carries herself, the way she speaks, and the way she writes.

Therefore, it is no surprise that Taliercio's writing reflects the spirits of others- everyone from a working class hotel worker who couldn't walk to work in the freezing temperature of Syracuse, to her cat Mr. Darin Tidaback who suffered from diabetes. Talierclo writes and shares stories with her care for spirits in mind. "I was in my twenties and I went to see a psychic. Her name was Grace Shapiro. I'll never forget it," Taliercio says in a moment of reflection, remembering a time years ago when she realized she was a writer.

"She told me what was going to happen to my grandmother. My grandmother worked in a girdle factory in the Bronx. She had bad hips and cataracts. She needed a walker. She went into the hospital in 1979 where she found out she had brain cancer. Around the time she went into the hospital, I visited Grace for guidance. The psychic told me to save everything- save all the bits and all the pieces because I'll need them. She said at 42 I'll become a writer. So I did, you know, save everything. And she was right. Only, just a little off." She pauses. "I was 51."

Though she says she officially became a writer at 51, the exact moment marked with her enrollment in a union-sponsored writing class led by Ester Cohen and Steve Parks, she's actually been a writer for much longer. Since elementary school with her favorite teacher Mrs. Webster, she felt the inkling for writing. At public high school in Yonkers, New York, she honed her skills. In college at the College of New Rochelle, she kept working on her writing and continued after graduation, when she traveled the world and kept a journal. By and by, she worked various waitress jobs at hotels – always saving things she owned, pieces she wrote and stories in her head.

Ann Marie moved to Syracuse at the end of 1983. Seven years later she took the job she still holds today, president of the UNITEHERE-Local 150 (UNITE, formerly the Union of Needletraders, Industrial and Textile Employees, and HERE, Hotel Employees and Restaurant Employees International Union). At the time of her inauguration, it was just HERE before it merged with UNITE in 1994. Within her daily duties, she negotiates labor agreements and handles grievances through arbitration. She oversees organizational financial records. She advocates for workers through community and political activism. She trains workers and organizes union events for them.

Ann Marie is the face and voice of UNITE-HERE- local 150.

Beyond the union, she remains heavily involved with labor issues. In addition to serving as the union president, she held positions as the Vice-President of the AFL_CIO (American Federation of Labor and Congress of Industrial Organizations) as well as the Chair of the Working Families Committee. She was also a board member and delegate of the Greater Syracuse Labor Council and served as a secretary and treasurer of the New York State Political Action Council of the HER union.

In the working world and in the union world, writing for Ann Marie felt different. She learned the reverse of creative writing. She learned how to write press releases, speeches, how to use contract language to negotiate contracts, how to make fliers, and more. Basically, her writing shifted from a creative outlet to the outline form trying to get her point across in as few words as possible. Writing became technical, functional, and practical. She said she set her spirits aside and buckled down.

But when she joined a Syracuse writing group for labor workers in 2005, the creativity she felt in her youth emerged once again. "It's all been there. But, I had to peel away at the layers of my life to get back to the creativity I had as a child. It comes with life experience," she says. "When I got into the writing group, I felt like a writer for the first time. When I look back, all the signs are there. The poems I wrote and won contests, the journals I wrote traveling in Europe- those are all signs. Still, if you said to me now, are you a writer? I'd say NO. But when I look back I think I was preparing myself to become the writer I am today."

Today, her writing spawns from two priorities in life: her work in the union and her belief in spirits. Ann Marie writes about the spirits of the people who she helps in the union and the spirits of her animals. She is currently at work on her children's book about her late dog Gypsy, who once, with much notoriety, stood on the picket line for a union protest against the management of the Hotel Syracuse. Here, she share her thoughts on writing and its influence on her life:

What role does writing play in your life?

"Somehow from what I write, I think it's going to help someone and help them to heal. I'm hoping that these are stories that have taught me how to understand and heal my own life. I think what I'm hoping for is that they'll help someone else in the same way and help them to heal their life. My concept of healing is to lose fears and advance the soul on a spiritual journey. Hopefully an earthly journey as well.

For example, all my animal stories are about healing. They really have taken me into situations, whether it's meeting people or something I had to do, they've been the guide through my life. For example, like the story about Matthew the cat. I mean the story about Matthew, you can't imagine. I met that woman who fed him, who changed over in the past four years as a welfare mother, now she owns her own house and has a full-time job and takes care of kids with social problems. She came from poor upbringing never graduated high school. I helped her transform her life from welfare mother to someone who respects herself more. I know she does. I've been able to help her. It's all because of Matthew.

She was crying a year ago because she had nowhere to live. The house she lived in was being restored, and she was evicted with no place to go. But she's living in a house now for less money than she was renting. She's creating a good life. That's been a gift to me because I help very few people I interact with. I always say you only help them for a moment. Sure they keep their job for another few years. But it's hard to handle situations."

Nick Pollard by Mary Gallagher (London)

Perhaps it is evening, and you find yourself in an average English pub. It's a little dingy on the outside, not especially striking against an evening sky threatening rain. A few low lights illuminate the pub from atop each rectangular table; it's a sleepy look that seems to compliment the fading sunlight of the day's slow end, while contrasting the crowd, recently finished with work, which has filled the space up with talk, laughter, and banter. It's another raucous night, and a perfect chance for Nick Pollard to introduce himself.

Nick Pollard loves the camaraderie of a pub as much as the camaraderie found in writing, especially the writing associated with marginalized communities. Though he would not necessarily categorize himself as working class, it's only because he has come "to regard class as an inadequate frame of reference." Regardless of labels, Pollard is familiar with what many might consider to be a working class lifestyle; he was raised in Swindon, an industrial town in Wiltshire in western England, and came from a family of teachers, freelance writers, railway office clerks, and tracers of engineering drawings.

In between several degrees (including ones from poly-technic in Communication Studies; a masters in Psychiatry, Philosophy, and Society; and an MSc in Occupational Therapy) made possible through government funding and his own pocket money, Nick has bounced amid a slew of odd jobs and tight paychecks. To close the gap between his working class experience and a more privileged education, Pollard began a habit that would fuel his interests for years afterwards: "I did feel different because I figured that everyone would somehow know more than me about life, everything. I decided to embark on a kind of voyage of self-discovery, which involved a lot of reading to acquire the sophistication I thought my contemporaries had." Pollard's growing appreciation for a good read was soon to fuel an interest in writer groups, education, and his career in occupational therapy.

Writing has always seemed to have a visible presence in Pollard's life. He has been involved with writer groups since 1980, when he joined Heeley Writers in Sheffield, England. For him, the Federation of Worker Writers and Community Publishers (FWWCP) has been a combination between a "vernacular university" and a "family." He explains that the FWWCP "opened the conceptual door that allowed me to see how ordinary experiences are significant, and how it is not just the lives of the great and the good who should be celebrated. History is not composed of a procession of presidents, kings and prime ministers, interspersed with a few explorers." The exchange of narrative experience that energizes the FWWCP workshops and writings is something he found pleasantly echoed in occupational therapy. Now a husband and a father, Nick has a library of books that threaten to overtake his house, and he continues to slip writing projects in amidst familial, teaching, and academic obligations.

Nick Pollard's words came to me from across the ocean, emailed in an unintentionally appropriate shade of aquamarine green. As his words reconstruct him for you, wherever you may be, I hope you'll imagine your interaction with his narrative in the setting he finds so ideal for these sorts of first impressions: "When we have visiting dignitaries and fellow academics, [they] all get taken to see Chatsworth House, which was featured in the Brideshead Revisited television series in the 1980s. I'm serious. If I get to be a visiting academic, I want to go to the pub, meet some ordinary people and drink some decent ale."

Interview with Nick Pollard

What role has writing played in your life?

Writing is something that you get to kind of nurse along like a kind of lump under your skin. I don't write all the time, and my academic writing has to some extent taken the place of the writing I like to do, which is poetry. Poetry is a kind of carpentry. Words have to be honed to fit and slapped into place and taken apart and refitted. This is playing about with words really. But I think they [words] have to reach something – it is an empty game unless they mean something more than the stuff on the page. One of my favourite songs is "Books are Burning" by XTC. This was about the Salman Rushdie protests, but it also relates to something that happened in Swindon, where XTC are from. In 1958, all twelve library copies of the Penguin translation of The Decameron were burnt after people complained that the contents were obscene. The song describes how books are people, a way of listening to the voices of the past in the present. Writing provides the opportunity to have a little word in someone else's ear, and when you read, it is as if they are talking personally to you, even if they are Herodotus from 2,500 years back. Books are weapons for change, too – people burn books because they are frightened by them. I'd like to write a book that was good enough to burn!

Audience is important to your writer, and thus to writing. It is a writer's job to reach an audience, to

inspire something within them. Does the audience have a role to fulfill when it comes to writing?

Well, the answer to this comes from one of the things that did stick with me from the polytechnic degree (in Communication Studies). Barthes wrote in The Pleasure of the Text that the audience is to react to the writing and strive for the interpretation is a phenomenological one, it will vary according to experience.

Of course- this is nothing to do with the commercial power of the publishing organisation to sell and disseminate writing. You don't have to look too far to find commercially produced writing of poor quality. But some people are reading it. I used to read a lot of science fiction and was also interested in the critical literature around this. One of the interesting debates concerned A Canticle for Leibowitz by Walter Miller, which reviewers had said was such a good book it wasn't science fiction but literature with a big L. There was a bizarre series of critiques following this, the strangest of which was by Michel Butor of the French Academy who proposed on the basis of a strange array of novels with a fantasy element in them that all science fiction writers should write about the same world which would be less confusing for the audience (maybe this is lost in the translation). Theodore Sturgeon came up with what was called Sturgeon's Law: 90% of science fiction is crap, but then 90% of everything is crap. Actually I don't know if this really does hold true of everything, but I suppose that the audience has to do a little work to find out what is good in what one reads.

How did you come to think of yourself as a writer?

I have wanted to write since I was about seven. I wrote on and off in my spare time and enjoyed creative writing at school. In fact, I had a couple of teachers- Mr. Hazel and Mr. Watson in particular- when I was about nine to ten years old who worked to encourage my junior class to appreciate poetry writing. My dad was an influence on this too: he was a writer, so I wanted to be one. There were lots of books in the house, I had a lot of books as a child, reading was encouraged, my parents both read to me from very early on; it was possible to be a writer, which is something that a lot of FWWCP writers have had to recognise for themselves without support- at least I didn't have that as an issue. But later I had to ask myself: was it possible for *me* to be one? Had I really got anything worth saying? Workshops are essential for finding out if that is true.

How do workshops help you- or writers in general- to improve writing?

I've just been rereading one of Tom Woodin's papers about the FWWCP. One of the points he makes about writing at the time of the 1980s, when there was a lot of separatism and debates about separatism in the left, was the way that people patronised writers who wrote badly: nobody wanted to criticise [other people's] writing in case they were thought to be criticising [these] people because they were women, black, or gay, or whatever. Not giving them criticism was a disservice, they would have benefited from a critical discussion which enabled them to develop their material. If the writer thinks they deserve respect simply because they are a writer, there is something amiss. You have to be disciplined and learn to hone your craft so that it can be used well.

It's always good to get feedback from your writing. Community writing offers many opportunities for instant feedback, and in the past I have had quite a lot of positive critical feedback about poems I've written. If your group has a critical focus and you are busy taking each others' work apart each week (which not everyone likes to do- it is a discipline and sometimes painful) you read other people's work with a critical eye, and you recognise that you can write too. I have found the FWWCP was a great place to learn the craft of writing, sharing writing, accepting criticism. This helps you to think about how you can improve technique, delivery, and style; you go and read other people and then you have a go at producing something similar, trying to get your own twist on it.

SECTION TWO:
HOLDING ON

Alonna Berry, Failure to Assimilate (USA)

I remember my first encounter with Syracuse University. It was on a college visit, I had been invited to compete in a Maxwell Scholarship program that my high school grades had earned me a spot in. My parents were so excited, I have to admit – I was too. I thought after being rejected from Yale and Dartmouth, being accepted in the top ten percent of the incoming class of Syracuse University wasn't bad – and if I got another scholarship it wouldn't have been that bad of a deal. Well anyway – back to the story. When I first walked up the stairs to Maxwell School of Citizenship – I thought, this is the place for me to be. As we all filed into the auditorium I began to think this may be a little harder than I thought. I wasn't surprised to see that I was maybe one of five African-American students there out of an auditorium of maybe 200 or so. This is what I was used to. Throughout my entire high school career if I wasn't the token "black kid," I was definitely always the token "black girl." So to say the least I felt right at home... Or at least I thought.

Even though I was used to my surroundings, I wasn't used to the atmosphere. Everyone looked at me differently. They even seemed surprised when I spoke – I couldn't understand. Suddenly it all seemed so foreign to me. I began to look around and nothing that I saw was familiar anymore. I began to feel so out of place, and then I felt my body begin to tremble. It was my turn to speak in front of the group for the competition. The topic was Immigration. Most of the people before me who had spoken simply said build a wall – we don't need any more foreigners in this country. They seemed so insensitive to me. Didn't they understand that immigration is what founded this country, and that most of the immigrants that cross the Mexico-America border don't tarnish our country – they are helping to rebuild it. I did not come from an immigrant family, but some my closest friends did and their parents have worked hard to build a home, and gain citizenship. I couldn't imagine what it could be like to live a life that close-minded.

Well that was just the beginning of my experience at Syracuse University. I later learned that there are many class, race, and social microcosms there. When I was 17, I started taking classes at Syracuse, in a SummerStart program. After visiting for my shocking scholarship competition I was surprised to see the vast difference in the students attending SummerStart. I was not the "token black girl or person" – in fact I was surrounded by more African American students then I had ever been in my life. Almost every person in the SummerStart program was a person of color. I had to admit I was excited, and astonished. I had never been in a learning or living situation like this before. When I walked into Watson Hall, and found my way up to the 2nd floor, room 204 (my key envelope said), I was the first one to arrive – so I began unpacking and decorating with my parents. This was going to be my new home for the next 6 weeks…

When we were almost finished unpacking I heard the door open, it was my new roommate. She came in with a man helping her who was not much older than us. After he moved her things in, they said goodbye and he left. I was surprised at how quickly he had left, but I didn't want to get in her way as she began to unpack her belongings. My parents and I decided that we should make our Wal-Mart run now to allow her to unpack. Before we left, I introduced myself, and asked her if she wanted us to pick her up anything from Wal-Mart. Surprisingly she responded, "I've never been to a Wal-Mart before, I don't really know what they have there." I didn't know what to say, where I am from, in the country-suburban community of Delaware, Wal-Mart was the pinnacle of everyone's being. I couldn't comprehend. In order to combat my confusion my mother said, "Well if you want to come along you're more than welcome." She agreed, and by this time our Chevy Suburban was now full with two other new students as we made our way to Wal-Mart. As we were driving I discovered a few things.

None of my "new friends" had ever been to Wal-Mart before, they were all from New York City, and their names were Shaquana (my roommate), Myranne, and David. David was Columbian, Myranne was Puerto Rican, and Shaquana was black like me. As we continued to drive I began to realize what a different environment college life was going to be. To me, Syracuse seemed like a big city; to them it seemed like the country.

I couldn't imagine a country with an interstate, freeways, and highways. I was dumfounded. I live on Woodlytown Road, across the street from a corn field in Magnolia, Delaware. This all seemed so foreign to me – not just the interstates, freeways, and streetlights, but the people too – the people were the most foreign of all.

As we made our way into Wal-Mart the absolute look of amazement on their faces astonished me (but my parents didn't seem so surprised). When everyone was finished shopping, we were on our way back to Watson Hall. When my dad pulled up the hill in our Big Blue Suburban, and pulled in front of the door of Watson to let us all out I knew what had just happened. I had just been labeled: "the uppity, rich black girl from Delaware or Maryland or something like that." The scary feeling began to come back, and even though like during the scholarship completion I was amongst my peers… this time I didn't stand out because of my skin, I stood out because of who I was. I talked different, I walked different, I dressed different – I was different.

Sometimes it's not just about race, it is about class too. As SummerStart came to an end, and I was chosen to give the speech at the ending ceremony – I talked about my experiences in SummerStart. I spoke about what I learned, and what we had to look forward to in a few weeks in August. The speech was hopeful and reflective – just like a good commencement speech should be. But I have to admit, as I stood on the stage, and looked at my audience I knew that an audience of my peers would never look so colorful again. As my hands began to tremble, and my body to shake, I wasn't nervous, I was fearful. Fearful of what I had saw in the scholarship competition, fearful or what I encountered in the Suburban my first day of SummerStart, I was fearful… because what I had done and would continue to do is fail to assimilate.

Natalie Pascarella, Untitled (USA)

You sit still

Stiff

Rigid as the walls that climb behind you

Walls plastered with portraits

Men of science, math and literature

They told you the men were important

They told you to learn their names

They told you to commit their words to heart

And to take their thoughts as truth

But for now

In this moment

Your only thoughts are your bones

And of their struggle to hold you upright

They are heavy lead pipes

At odds with the smooth contours of your wooden desk

You notice how the others sit with ease

How they raise their hands as if they were feathers

But your hands are too heavy to lift

A woman stands

Paces

Her mouth moves in rhythm less motion

And the drone she spins makes you think of the factory

Where machines buzz and whir in mindless constancy

You realize the factory is your place

Where your time and your body are your gifts

Gifts that you are forced to give

And which are never returned

The clock ticks

Steady

You follow the second hand with your eyes

A bell rings out and the crowd surges

Up and out and away

Only you remain as the walls crumble into plaster puddles

Replace themselves with colder, grayer walls

Walls without portraits

Walls that house the whir and buzz of machines

There are no men of science here

Svetlana Sagaidak, On the Panopticon (UK)

Could not resist to put my sketches in rhyme, –

If it would be my will, I would not limit my writing to line

But academic standards dictate parameters to despair

I'm still a beginner in this vertical affair

So, I beg you, don't judge my rhetoric severe... so there

Life in plastic – it's fantastic

Time in bubble – gives no trouble

Mind under taper – safer than fire a fighter

Build with clouds, why use bricks?

Dreams, nightmares – all dig deep

Combinations form new styles

No need for overreaction – it's all in the fraction

Fantasies with marble motion arise through the hands

Non-testaceous creatures, just pretend you understand

Shells' reflection in the Skies, spiroid essence multiplied

Antidotes to reaction stored on a dusted shelf

Why new ideas? Drifts, axioms will equilibrate

Internal obsessions cause morality, normality…

Adjusted docility set on high visibility

How arbitrary the absence of individuality

Christine W., Untitled (USA)

It's a funny thing, being a poor kid in a wealthy school district. You become aware of the difference as early as elementary school. Everyone invites you to their birthday parties at the gymnastics center or Chuck E. Cheese and all you can offer is some grocery store cupcakes during class. Maybe you decide that you were born to be a singer, or a soccer player, but your parents tell you there's no money for lessons or uniform fees. So you decide that you're at least born to read books and your parents oblige you with as many secondhand Nancy Drew mysteries as they can. You think it's cool that your dad is a carpenter and helps to build houses, but you tend to avoid those "what does your father do" conversations where everyone's dad is a lawyer, doctor or otherwise rich guy.

By middle school you start to get these bitter notions of just how poor you are. Your family doesn't own a summer cottage or a motorboat, so you must be really poor. You don't take a yearly trip to Florida during mid-winter break and you've never been anywhere remotely Disney. You're one of the only kids who buys her lunch at school, and only pays a quarter for it to boot. Your friends don't really get the whole reduced price lunch thing, and you sullenly decline to enlighten them about it.

In high school you're too busy with your homework, activities and part time job to think much about how poor you are. Sometimes you remember, like when your mom has to teach you to drive instead of learning in a driver's education class, or when your classmates are getting ready for the SAT in a prep class. You probably could have paid for classes with your job money, but you're saving up for a car. You just hope it won't be the ugliest car in the student parking lot...although it might be the rustiest.

And then you get to college (where your financial aid is very good to you). You take some classes for your liberal arts core and have a brief stint as a tutor in the city school district, and, boy, then you know what poor is, and it isn't you. Turns out that the fact that your parents were able to own that little house in the suburbs means you're not that poor. Your family is covered by basic health insurance through your dad's employer, and you can't recall ever going hungry at dinnertime.

You like the term "working class;" it describes you better than "poor" did. "Working class" accounts for the comforts you enjoyed and the opportunities that were available, and doesn't disrespect the realities faced by those who are truly "poor." As graduation nears and you're contemplating your launch into the real world, you finally unashamedly appreciate that you were a working class kid in that wealthy school district. You're thankful for the top-notch education, and also for the humility and perspective gained in making do with limited means. As you don that silly gown and perform the ceremonious march into adulthood you just hope that you can pass along that perspective to your children.

Vanessa Davis, Untitled (USA)

I.

today is just

another day I showed up for

another day of busy

another day of bore

another day that I just showed up

to watch simple things turned into riddles

straight lines made into knots

the same hard things always come as a surprise,

bumps tripped over, and over again

another day to be disengaged

another day to keep it that way

(please, don't invent another noose

to tie me to your chores)

another day in silenced rage

at myself of the life I sell

for a paltry prize (and a damned good

benefits package, I must add)

another day I wonder about my Creator's outrage

for each day I stay and do nothing else

another day I'm paid to circulate the dough

to keep the wheels turning

to keep it all going:

the rent/food/and car

the local economy

get my nails done

buy Connie's Mary Kay

II.

another day of hope

that I can give of my substance

to bring means and hope across an ocean

and know it thrives in Kenya

another day of mercy

another day of grace

another day to see life born again

in an extinguished heart

another day to remember who I am

another day to identify myself again

to sweep the cloak of worldly sadness aside

to lay down my armor or argument

another day to step into God's presence

in all nakedness

from pretense

III.

another day I walk through the gate

into the garden within me

and think of what lies beneath the hardened ground

another day I look, then turn away

from the work that needs to be done

of digging (and I hate digging-when all I have is a spoon)

the treasure, right here, conveniently buried

and now I got to dig it up

another day lost to Work

the work I need to do seems dim some days

as if I've forgotten how

another day lost not to "Work"

but to jobs strung along a path

much the same flavor, texture and hue

long ago, as is now, tickets and tales were sold

I bought the one that brought me on this trip

of showing up

at places that would have me

do things

others will set before me to do

hire myself out-my hands and my back

skills I've learned for the job

convinced to leave my field fallow

just to always have something to "fall back on"

only to always be fallen back

and wonder

what is to become of my field?

today is another day

I showed up

and gazed through the gate

of my own inner garden

another day towards the trail

another day a glance behind

just another repeat

of the day before

Steve Oakley, No Right to Write (UK)

I an't got no right to write

Cos evrythin I do is shite

I cant make my words fit

      into a neat rhyme

And novels just take too bloody long

I tried once you knowst

Wrote me life story, took nearly a week

An I typed it out all nice n neat

An posted it to London to a big book

Company but it must ave got lost

So a year later

I was visiting my sister there

I took a copy to the building

      on the address

An spoke to a bloke at the front desk,

he were a right ponce

He says to me I need an appointment

That I had to leave,

And calls over this handy looking

  security guard

Name on the badge says Steve

He looks pretty hard

So I make my way to the door

An ah says to him

"What they treating people like

that for? He inna bad sort after all

An he says to me,

"I guard the building mate,

but they guard British culture 'rate"

I didna ave a fuckin clue

What'd just happened

And that was ma writin days done

I gave up there n then

I an't got time for smarmy gits

I went back home n called it quits-

  put telly on

But ah can wax lyrical

An I no all the big words

I use em to confuse em

Dine at the Birds – that's ma local

ENCOUNTERS

Encounters

Roy Birch, The Federation of Worker Writers visit to the USA –
November 2006.

What I am about to recount happened some three and a
half years ago and I have a notoriously bad memory, so I
am going to reference myself from Nick Pollard's diary of
the events. I hope my reflections won't seem wooden or
crass. Apologies in advance in case they do.

In November 2006, Tim Diggles, Nick Pollard, Rosie
Garland, my wife Lucia, and I made a five-day visit to
the USA to work with Steve Parks, Associate Professor of
Writing and Rhetoric and some of his students at Syracuse
University in New York State, as part of an initiative to study
the impact of class on education and literature.

At Manchester Airport we quickly ran into a spot of bother
on account of Lucia's request to be allowed to take her
guitar with her on the plane as hand luggage. The man
at the check-in desk was not impressed but eventually
gave his permission. This, for me, was the precursor to
eight hours of terrified boredom, which I all too frequently
exacerbated by gazing out upon a ridiculously large amount
of extremely deep and extremely distant water.

We eventually arrived over a considerable land-mass which I recognized as America because I could see a lot of Baseball Diamonds. And then we were at Newark Airport and I was safe again.

Newark Airport was fun. Nick failed to complete the necessary paperwork and was almost refused entry to the fabled Land of the Free, following which, my fingerprints, for reasons known only to the Devil's intricate sense of humour, crashed the entire Homeland Security computer system, which caused a significant, though happily short-lived panic.

Short-lived though the panic was, our group was now a major focus of attention. I was with Lucia. Lucia had big hair and a guitar. Homeland Security, in a desperate attempt to restore a sense of parity to the situation, homed in on the guitar.

"Why are you taking a guitar to a writers' conference?"

"I write songs."

Mike Tyson could not have done it better. A perfect one-punch knock-out. Homeland Security capitulated. We were allowed through. The Fed was in America.

That evening we took part in a poetry evening in Manhattan, at the Peace House on the corner of Lafayette and Blecker, as guests of New York Poetry Collective The Bread is Rising. It was a wonderfully friendly and stimulating event with lovely people and some extremely collectable poetry. This was Fed territory without a doubt. The Bread is Rising is a group with strong local connections and proud to be so. Fighters for the rights of the disadvantaged, of whom there are all too many in that locality. One of the group, Sabir Mohammed, is a rat exterminator. He, and another group member, Schmm (Sr Amn Ra Schmm Khnuu – yes, you heard), had to leave early – they work night shifts. Great poets, great people, very humbling to meet them. But that night it wasn't just them and us. A third group was represented – Precious Promise Arts Circle, from Brunswick, New Jersey. The group is based around a Church Community and their work has a strong religious representation while at the same time being very concerned with social issues – theirs is the very same community Paul Robeson hailed from. I came away feeling I had been accorded a huge privilege – contact with a realer and truer America - which left me in awe of the integrity of its struggle, and the realization of just how much courage life in the Home of the Brave demands of all too many of its residents. Our journey to Manhattan also gave me one of my abiding memories of the USA – being stuck in a gargantuan tailback at the entrance to the Holland Tunnel.

The following day (Sunday) we set off for Syracuse and I experienced my first encounter with another of my abiding memories of America – the American Diner. American Diners are a joy to the soul. Great food, wonderful coffee, pancakes with Maple Syrup. Incredible.

Monday morning saw us begin the working part of our trip, a breakfast meeting at Syracuse University with local union members and Steve's director of studies, over donuts and coffee. Many of the people we spoke with are involved in the development of literacy for low-paid workers, poor literacy being one of the major obstacles they face with regard to obtaining better-paid work. We obviously have the same problem in Britain, but somehow it feels quite scarily more intense over here.

Monday morning also provided me with yet another of my abiding memories of the United States. Syracuse University sits atop a high hill and is fronted by two of the finest pieces of American Gothic architecture that anyone could wish to see.

More meetings – with Georges Marceau and Terry Ritchie of the 1199SEIU health workers union, with Steve's writing class, with university staff, with student classes, a meeting to discuss the Transatlantic Fed Book, an absolutely beautiful poetry evening at the Second Story bookshop, where needlessly apprehensive students did themselves and literature proud with their performances and were wonderfully appreciative of what we, as the Fed representatives, brought to the occasion, and where I discovered and purchased John Kennedy Toole's brilliant novel, A Confederacy of Dunces, and encountered what undoubtedly will always be my most abiding memory of America – Terry Ritchie's painfully haunting story about looking forward to being taken for a meal at a restaurant by her grandfather, but, when they got there, because of the segregation laws, being forced to eat out back sitting on crates. I confess to weeping surreptitiously, both at the injustice of the situation and the beauty of the telling.

Next day we left for Philadelphia, but not before visiting the ultimate eating house – Mother's Cupboard, a wooden shack on waste ground near the railway, where people queue for some of the best home cooking you will ever encounter, especially the Fritata, a mix of meats, vegetables, and scrambled egg, a meal so vast that anyone who finishes their plateful has their picture posted on the wall in the Mother's Cupboard Hall of Fame. Viva L'America.

In Philadelphia I encountered two more of my abiding memories of the US – a black ghetto the like of which is not found in Britain, and Steve's TV, the largest edifice of its kind that I have ever seen.

So much happened in so short a time that I have not been able to record anything close to all of it. It was a wonderful trip and much good work was done. Twice as long would have been three times as useful, but life is what it is and we get what we are given.

I loved what little I saw of America, that land of all-too-often terrifying contrasts, at that time still in the grip of the Bush regime. I loved the coupling of near-outlaw warmth and idealistic naivety that I encountered, and the realization it brought to me that the Fed and what it stands for are vital. The projects, the principles, and the writing the Fed inspires can teach us all so much about who and what we are and about the humanity within us. That the transatlantic link is still alive and functioning does credit to all concerned, most especially Tim Diggles and Steve Parks, who set it up. We need each other and what we can teach each other. That we have each other is beautiful. Long may it continue

The Fed

Victoria Arnold, Syracuse Writers visit to the UK

When Professor Steve Parks presented the opportunity to attend a conference in London with local writers, I did not fathom that I would be taking a trip that renewed my passion for education, advocacy, the arts, community, and also my faith in people to be more than what society values in them. The Fed, in other words, was awesome.

Our last day in London was spent from 9am-8pm with the Fed, and I loved every minute of it. Alicia, Alonna, Jesse and myself arrived an hour before opening the conference and helped set up sandwiches, drinks, salads and got to know some of the members of the Fed. We were greeted with smiles and happy exchanges from people who had driven long distances and prepared massive amounts of food for the afternoon. They were amazed that we came from Syracuse for the conference and even more amazed that we were not jetlagged. I immediately felt right at home. No pretenses, no snobbishness.

Here I was relaxed because everyone showed respect and admiration in others. They saw each other as organic beings that have grown as writers and artists who express themselves and against all adversity. I was especially touched by the Survivors Writing network. To me, they successfully embodied what it meant to support one another mentally, artistically and socially.

My workshops for the morning and afternoon were what I initially categorised to Steve Parks as "the free-spirited hippie ones". I was excited to express myself through writing, art, and undergo a Japanese Reiki treatment that unravels suppressed emotions. After my first workshop where we wrote a story and then sketched, coloured or painted it to life, I understood that this is more than writing. It was therapy. I came to know people through their joys, sorrows, struggles, triumphs, and open spirit. One woman who battled cancer, physical abuse and depression painted a scene on canvas about the birth of her son being her salvation and reason to live. Growing up around my mother who is an artist and oil painter, I noticed that she naturally possessed and harnessed painting skills. She had no formal education on styles and art forms but was an artist none the less. The work she produced was profound and touching. I could absorb her pain and embody her joy. It was extraordinary how writing can change an entire way of life for some people.

My next workshop was an experience that struck deeper than I expected but then I began to accept that this conference would have that effect. The Reiki was performed by an older gentleman named Roy who told me to relax. While I was nervous to undergo the ritual I couldn't believe how it opened up feelings and emotions I had long suppressed. I don't know if my preparation and understanding of what was to happen affected the process but I am certainly happy that I had this moment with the people from the Fed.

After spending two workshops together, having lunch and listening to poetry together I got to know quite a few people that I can never forget. Their open and dedicated spirits shone through in their words, and of course in writing.

SECTION THREE:
WORKING DAYS

Kay Ekevall, Education (UK)

At school, I knew history:

Kings and Emperors

Battles and heroes

There was something called

The White Man's burden

We seemed to do well under it,

But the black man didn't.

I didn't know about

Miners and dockers:

Their work and their battles,

I did hear about Peterloo

But those Chartists were bloodthirsty rebels,

They had to be put down!

My education began when I met

The hunger marchers from Aberdeen and Dundee

On their way to London

David Kent, Priceless (USA)

In 1982, while in high school looking forward to graduation, my world as I knew it crashed and burned. I was told by educators I could not graduate based on my competencies, which were under state education requirements for graduation at the time. "You will have to stay back another year to make them up."

Well, at the time the United States President was Ronald Regan, who signed a bill that basically said you must be enrolled in college curriculum by the age eighteen in order to keep receiving social security disability benefits on my mother's behalf. Mom was disabled physically by then. We could not afford to lose her SSD benefits or we would lose everything. I could not allow this to happen. So, without any college prep classes and no high school diploma, I had to enroll in a college curriculum at Onondaga Community College (OCC). I wanted to enroll in an electronics technology program at OCC. The program had been filled for two years and there was a waiting list, but based on my entrance exam I was put at the bottom. Yes- a very low exam score. Again, I said to myself, "Damn, where do I go from here? Enroll in another curriculum or what?"

So I swallowed my anger and my stress, and went to go talk to my advisor. She suggested that I consider a humanities program for now, until an opening in my choice program occurred. After a bout of self-doubt, I said I'm going to do it. Boy, was I stupid. The study of the human mind, I didn't even make matriculation (the grade point average). The best I received was a 1.9 (of a 4.0 scale). I had 10% participation in this class!

By May 1982, I was out, and wondering how I was going to pay back a $1,700 school loan. Higher education services knew. At a 1982 education and vocation seminar, I met with Karl and May Knowlton. They operated the industrial work division at Olsten Temporary Services. While under a lot of stress, I approached and asked what types of temporary employment they offered.

"We have industrial labor position right now," they said. So I figured with my background as a laborer I had a good chance of getting a pretty good job with Olsten Temporary Services. For once, I was right.

They had a position opening for a industrial laborer at Bristol Myers Squibb Company, a very large international pharmaceutical business. They offered me a temp assignment for about one year on the third shift, which gave me time to plan ahead and start an active full time employment search and access those employment and training programs available for dislocated workers, which I was at the time. Even knowing I would not receive a great employment opportunity, I still pounded the pavement, read the classified ads daily in the Syracuse Herald-Journal, and bussed the distance to the suburban Syracuse area or where a classified might take me. Still, I never gave up the search; being an optimist permits me to do that. Perseverance was my partner.

I stayed with Olsten Temporary Services until June 1985 in different areas of industrial employment. Yes, I did return to Bristol Labs to various positions. All I knew is that I was receiving a weekly paycheck that helped my family's economic hardship. I was very thankful for this opportunity.

Let's remember the important issues in my life are about being from a working class family and, yes, my relationship was much different than those who are privileged to have two working parents and are able to have the finances to afford a good education. I do not have a chance to return to school in the future. What matters to me is to make sure that my mother is able to pay our monthly responsibilities without falling under. Through this sacrifice in my life, it was all worth it and if I had to, I would do it all again. The lessons I learned as a youngster and in working helped to bring money into the home to make sure there was food on the table and a roof over our head. To sacrifice this and to persevere- there is a light at the end of the tunnel. Just walk forward to the next step and soon enough you'll be there. Don't give up. If you fall, get up and keep walking. Strive to survive. Look at me. I made it. I did not stop. I kept my chin up and my feet in front of me.

I have my own responsibilities now. I am happily married and gainfully employed, handling life's financial responsibilities a day at a time and ready at a moment's notice to handle my family's financial occurrences as they happen- which has not happened for quite some time. Most importantly, a true statement that stands with me twenty four hours a day: family comes first.

I can only see a good ending to come to add to this collection of my life. As a young man who has struggled through education, earned an hourly wage at an early age, who had an alter ego who loved to dance and drink and have fun, I have matured into a hardworking, responsible man, with a voice for change, a workforce leader with recognition as a voice for organized workforces.

"In order to be the 'man', you have to beat the man." As an SEIU 1199 delegate and political organizer and activist, I have proven my character time and time again. My voice was heard in Albany, N.Y. in the largest rally in the history of labor organizing; it was myself along with 37,000 of my brothers and sisters from SEIU 1199 on April 1, 2001- a day I will never forget. Being forced into the labor force at an early age made me responsible, struggling through education made me a survivor, and dancing and moonlighting gave me a personality. Building a family made me a man. Being a member of SEIU 1199 gave me a voice and made me a leader. Working for a living and earning a wage made me an adult. It led me to having all this today, a job, a loving family, a workforce leader, waking up every day. This is for me, simply put, PRICELESS.

Roxanne Bocyck, A Capitalist Fairy Tale (USA)

Not so long ago in a place not too far away there was a society where a hard day's work earned you a fair wage. The war had ended. Jobs were plentiful. And a baby boom set into motion the building of automobiles, houses and government programs. Unions were strong and men with strong backs helped companies profit. And that was okay. College was for doctors and lawyers, scientists and engineers, politicians and presidents. The working class before this new generation of workers didn't need an education to make a living, and neither did this one. Or so they believed.

Communication was limited in this land of the free and the brave. No fences meant good neighbors. Police were present and people felt safe. The memories of The Great Depression still haunted their minds so they paid cash and hid their money under the mattress. It was a kingdom full of hopes and dreams. People learned to go without that which they couldn't afford. Those who had wealth didn't show it for they didn't want to pay the tax man. Everyone appeared equal and that is how it should be.

One day a child was born into this thriving capitalistic society. She didn't have a silver spoon but instead she lived in a 12 x 60 foot silver trailer. Her parents didn't finish high school but they graduated into marriage and a family. He

worked the swing shift and she rocked the baby to sleep. They owned a Dodge powerwagon, warm clothes, and always had food on the table. Before they knew it their only child went to school and Mom went to work making pocketbooks in a small factory that is now a restaurant named The Spaghetti Warehouse. Dad would drink and the little girl became afraid. She never knew if her father would come home drunk or sober. Life was so uncertain in this capitalistic society. She would pray and cry herself to sleep holding a blonde curly-haired doll that peed her pants when the girl gave her a bottle of water in a tiny hole between her lips.

The years went by and the family grew. Grandparents died and the trailer became too small. They didn't know any rich people so they didn't know any better way of life. Neighbors lived in bigger, newer, more colorful trailers. Mom got a new job as a bartender at the bar two miles down the road. It was here she helped the working class feel happy and forget about the uncertainty. They would leave her tips while dad worked the swing shift and the little girl now played mother to her younger siblings. Dad decided to build an addition but he never finished it. The family fell apart and the building stopped.

Mom found a man who owned a motorcycle and Dad left for Texas. Now the new family moved to a small village of brick apartments with paved parking lots and cable television. The new dad worked at a factory that made air conditioners where overtime wages bought new furniture and a new life. His two children from a previous marriage would come to visit on the weekends. He paid his child support of $20 a week while the dad in Texas paid none. Life was as it should be for a man in this capitalistic society: a decent wage, health insurance, and retirement.

As the young girl became a young lady she wanted what her Barbie dolls and television shows told her she should have: a husband to take care of, children who loved her, and a house to call a home. But one day in high school she heard a new word: college. It seemed college was full of opportunities for women to have a career and not depend on a man to take care of them. She couldn't wait to get home and tell her 40-hour-a-week, remarried, and now secure working mother about this new word she had learned at school. She patiently waited in her room looking over the papers the school had given her earlier that day for her mother to fill out.

At last she was home.

"Mom," the girl eagerly waited for her mom to stop flipping splattering burgers in a pan.

"Tonight at school they're having a meeting for high school kids who want to go to college and …"

But before she could finish -- her mom laughed -- without even taking her eyes off of the stove, "College? You're not going to college! We can't afford for you to go to college."

The girl stood there, hiding the papers from her school behind her back, not knowing what to say next. She had anticipated her mother wanting to help her become something more than a woman who was expected to marry and have children. But instead her mother opened the oven and checked on the french fries.

And that was that. The clock read 5:00 and soon her step-father who had been at work since 5:00 a.m. would be home. Mom needed to finish cooking dinner and told the girl to quit standing there and go set the table. Oh, and could she make sure there was mustard on the table because he likes mustard on his hamburger. So the girl did as her mother said. How would she become a teacher if she didn't go to college?

She graduated from high school and won an award for her school work but it wasn't enough to send her to college, but it was enough to fix her boyfriend's car. And it would be that car that brought their baby home from the hospital. And it would be that car that took her husband to work as a mechanic where he used his hands to provide for his family while she rocked the baby to sleep. They would live in a 14 x 70 foot sage trailer with white shutters and a wooden deck where they could barbeque. She had a high school diploma and he didn't graduate, just like his parents before him. He was taught all a man needed was a strong back and an honest day's work to survive. Life was good; life was as it should be.

As the years passed, the mother of two went to work to help provide for her family. She found a job working the second shift at a china factory with decent pay and health benefits. She didn't like being away from her children at night. Her step-father lost his job at the factory that made air conditioners but the workers got a settlement from the union. Meanwhile, her husband went from job to job, frustrated with his inability to find work that provided decent pay and health benefits for an honest day's work. They wanted to buy a home but the bank required five-years of steady employment and 5 percent down. So she was stuck at a job that left her tired and angry while her husband decided to start his own business which added to his self-worth as a man. She longed for a higher paying career that fulfilled her as a person. But the ones in the paper she liked required a college degree.

She thought the only way for her family to enter a new class of this capitalistic society was to make more money. Her husband's business was prospering and she wanted to attend college, but how could she make it happen? Education is not free; it is something people pay for as a society to participate in. One day she has had enough. How could she go to college if she never tried?

In a classroom, integrity helps people rise to the top. Motivation comes from within, not from a paycheck. College gives each person a voice. College is a different type of struggle; it's not the money as much as it is self-worth. Her husband becomes jealous of the time it takes away from him and their home for his wife to attend college. But her desire to become someone she can be proud of is stronger than his desire for her to give up. Now their children are grown and one already has two years of college.

One day while cooking a hamburger she remembers the conversation with her mother all those years ago in the kitchen. She wants her mother to be proud of her accomplishments like going to college on her own.

But her mother still laughs as she drinks her whiskey and collects social security. Her stepfather sips his gin while he opens his retirement statement and watches television. To them, life is good; life is as it should be. Their class of capitalism is about to fade away creating a new struggle for those who follow.

Danielle Quigley, Server (USA)

Perhaps you have seen her

Rushed and flustered

Belittled and beaten down

Forcing smiles

With strained politeness

Biting her tongue?

Perhaps you mock her

"Ignorant profession"

A server tending to your needs

Her trite existence

With meager means-

A lifestyle unlike your own

Perhaps you pity her

"Oh look she's pregnant!"

"And so young!"

Quick, ring check-

"at least she's married..."

Poor baby

Or perhaps you are her-

Struggling, hardworking

A college student with honors

A writer with potential

A happily married woman

An excited mother-to-be

Perhaps if you saw me

As more than a server

Grant me the credit I merit

Dispose of your pity or mockery-

Recognize the resemblance?

Could I be you?

Pat Dallimore, Mum's Writing (UK)

Sit down be quiet read a book

Don't you dare to speak or look

Shush Mum's writing

She's left the dishes in the sink

All she does is sit and think

Shush Mum's writing

Nothing for dinner now for tea

And all she ever says to me is

Shush Mum's writing

But what's all this Mum's wrote a book

Why not buy one have a look

No need to shush now we can shout

And tell all our friends about

MUM'S WRITING

Vera Beaton, Girls (USA)

I guess I'm a feminist. I don't really know. I used to attend some meetings, but would frequently start to disassociate when the discussion would turn to middle class concerns.

1986

Cassandra ends the lecture with: "We will have a better impact on controlling the stereotypical images of women when cable television is universally available." Cassandra was a potter. She was a Marxist-feminist. Her husband taught sociology at a local university. The room full of "womyn" in hippie-casual attire applauded this insight. I floated to the top of the room and tried to resist the overwhelming urge to speak ... oh no, vocal cords vibrating... sound coming out... I zoom back to my body on the last notes of "And we'll ensure everyone has a TV, HOW?" (Just sit, listen and TRY to learn, Minerva. My mantra fails me once again. Must be time for a new mantra, I guess.) An embarrassing silence follows my outburst. I was being the poor white-trash-single-mother again. I was on welfare, taking a philosophy degree on an Ontario Student Assistance Program (a SAP) loan after quitting my job at the chip truck. Why couldn't I be more comfortable to be around?

I decided, for a time, that I had more in common with working class men than middle class women.

1991

I coach soccer at my daughter's school between part-time jobs and school. We're in the United States on a three-month visitor pass that expired in June of 1987. Some might say "illegal alien," but I prefer the term "documentation challenged."

(Too bad the Jamaican musicians on the Maple Leaf Express traveling out of Toronto, blowing on their brass instruments and happy to have a gig in "Noo Yark," didn't realize the importance of laying low, smiling sweetly, offering brief acceptable responses. They diverted the custom officials' attention from us, and I hope that they're rewarded for their sacrifice. They saved our lives.)

On the side lines of the soccer field, I mingle with some stay-at-home mothers. They're discussing working mothers. The Mother Hens cluck:

"I don't think they realize how important these early years are."

"My husband and I decided, after our first was born, that I'd be home full time ..."

"Some people are TOO greedy... they want all the toys ... I'd rather be THERE for my kids..."

(I start doing my mantra... it works (!), but maybe that's because I've changed it to: Shut up, Minerva, don't take it personally. They don't know. How could they know?) I smile, and turn my attention back to the kids running ...

1992

Deciding I need a pack, I send a photocopy invitation out to many women of my acquaintance. It reads: COME JOIN THE MADISON WOMEN'S BOWLING TEAM AND TERRORIST SOCIETY.

There was a survey where all the pre-formed responses were silly, absurd, or mind-numbing, along with a date for the first meeting. Well let me have some of that, on wry!

I had 10 women at the first meeting. We laughed and had coffee and snacks and talked about our expectations from the group. I volunteered to host the first event: The *Lingerie* Party.

A very nice lady comes to your house with catalogues and samples. You fill out a survey with questions about your fantasies, self perceptions and experiences. There's a gift for those with the highest and lowest scores. I get the lowest, with two points less than my 11 year-old daughter.

"Hey, how could THAT be? I've actually HAD sex..., ha ha ha."

We all laugh. No one ever sees me with a man (or women either-don't THINK that question didn't come up!). How can I explain that I'm just too damn tired to care about myself in that way? We try on the samples, and laugh at ourselves, and purchase pretty/sexy underthings according to our tastes. My cat decides to defecate in a house plant to protest the noise and confusion. We laugh and laugh and laugh.

We have three, four, five more meetings, at different homes. We're getting more familiar with each other and there is less consensus. The topic of abortion comes up at a meeting. We all have our own points of view. People cry.

Our sixth meeting occurs at the home of my best girlfriend ('Best Friend'). She's eight years older than I am, and at the time, been divorced for seven years. She has three children, one of whom is developmentally disabled. Only five women come to the meeting/party. I ask someone if the abortion thing turned people off. There were non-committal answers and a deft change of subject. We sit on the floor of the family room and chatter while the warmth of a wood stove lulls us. The room smells good, and 'Best Friend' is charming us all with her food, her comfortable ways, and her gracious laughter.

After the meeting, in the driveway, a woman confides in me and says "I didn't expect her home to be so nice." I realize that although this woman had known my friend most of her life, she had never been in her house. Hmmm. I asked this woman what had happened to the other "terrorists." She explained: "Well, some of the women - their husbands wouldn't let them come. My husband told me, 'if I came here, people would think I was a "whore" because everybody knows how "Best Friend" is.' I told him to screw off!" she finished proudly.

(Holy cow...did I just get warped into a bad movie from the 60s? Beam me up, Scottie!)

1995

English 101 in nursing school. My door-to-door philosopher career is in tatters. Our professor is 23, male, and a newly-converted Catholic. I ask him if changing your religion is like transsexualism, changing what you're born with to meet your self-identity. He responds with a delighted "Yes!" (I get too playful with these concepts, sometimes, but I've tried not to lie.) He's a good teacher. He asks interesting questions. We discuss the use of 'vile' images in stories and poetry. (Oh I love words, yes I do, with my dictionary all coffee stained and ragged,)

I write my first, and probably last, poem. I entitle it Girls.

Girls

Bad girls 'do' guys in the alleyway

Good girls hear about it later

Then they're shocked

Good girls have movie dates

Bad girls watch them drive by

They're standing on some corner

Bad girls talk about how big guys' dicks are

Good girls don't

But they wonder

Good girls make great babysitters

Bad girls get driven home by the mothers

No use taking any chances

Bad girls bowl

Good girls play field hockey

Athletics are so important

POLITICS

Bryan McGurk, Restorative Just Us (USA)

It had been so quiet before; cows, plains, families, a village.

Then they came from ravaged lands with blood upon their hands and hunger in their eyes.

They asked for what was not theirs to have.

Milk, cattle, you see are not wealth or trade items for us, it is our blood, the link between ourselves and the land, do you understand?

It was what allowed them to live as they did, it was why they had not abandoned the old ways and moved to cities, or armed themselves and turned in on their neighbors for food.

I got out of my way to say this because I want you to know that we are warriors and do not take such demands on our resources lightly, and as generous as we may be, like you, we would only feed those who asked for food, not demand it.

They were declined and turned away, peacefully, without a word.

That was how they returned that night, while those in the village slept quietly without saying a word.

That night they did not grant their victims the mercy that they were given that same day and left only death in their path.

I am telling you this because I was away that night, out with the cattle a half-day's wall from the village, and returned home the next day.

I gathered others, from other villages, and went to the office and we asked, we asked for the tool to make it right, the tool that was promised to us by our name and birthright.

I gave my name, I received my rifle.

Now the village clothesline looks different with no laundry, just the severed ears to remind us to listen carefully to those outsiders that come, and a message to outsiders: the same color that inspired fear in lions themselves would be known and feared amongst men for the same mighty warrior spirit.

We do not all take our rifles to the office anymore, and we watch for those with hunger in their eyes.

Roger Mills, Ban Fascism (UK)

It is written in huge four-foot letters. It can be seen clearly streets away.

It is a white paint daubing on a high brick wall which shouts BAN FASCISM.

It has been there ever since I can remember that's almost twenty years.

Its' paint is now beginning to fade. I remember seeing it when I had no conception of the word's meaning, and I remember not asking my parents in case it was something rude.

It is unfortunate that I ever did grow up to know what it meant, that it should be a word still relevant in the modern world.

Maybe it was scrawled up there by two young Jews with a brush and bucket of paint at the time of the Mosely street riots. I can almost see them in the dark night slapping on the paint carefully but quickly and all the time keeping a watchful eye on the empty streets.

Having finished their night's labour I imagine them running off into the dark not daring to look at the slogan until the following morning when along with a hundred others they could tut and gasp at the cheek of the graffiti artist's work.

"Who could have done such a thing", they would say mockingly and sharing a grin. There's a funny thing about that sign. If you stand very close to the wall it's just lines and circles. It tells you nothing. Yet just by standing back a few yards its message is very clear.

Sometimes one must be free of oppression to understand that he has been oppressed.

But what of them now? What of the brave hotheads who felt they could not live that night through without advertising their emotions. Are they still as heated and eager to alight the world or have the drops of time extinguished the flame. Maybe they are tired and apathetic, maybe they are dead. No matter if they are either. For a little while at least they have left a tribute to the people they were and the politics of compulsion.

The work of those graffiti artists is as deep and honourable as anything hanging in the National Gallery. Maybe more so. It doesn't belong in a museum though but where it is in the streets. Its audience is you and me. It is a plea and a warning.

Pray the fading white paint need never be renewed.

SECTION FOUR: FUTURE ACTIONS

The Trans-Atlantic Worker Writer Federation Manifesto

1. Education should teach a global humanity (not the humanities) based on an alternative sense of history and where cooperative values and restorative justice are primary.

2. Education should take place in a safe environment free from traditional social/economic biases with self-respect for each other as individuals as well as members of different classes, heritages, and sexualities.

3. All educators must move from subconsciously teaching students to be Westernized versions of "them" to teaching the essential equality among all individuals and cultures.

4. The conceptual equality taught to students must also be manifested in equal funding and equal access to well-maintained school facilities.

5. To base an educational system on any other values accepts a fundamental inequity in society and acceptance that now all human potential will be fulfilled.

APPENDIX

Original Members of the Trans-
Atlantic Worker Writer Manifesto

Brendan Abel
Lynne Ashburner
Dave Chambers
Melodie Clarke
Eric Davidson
Joan DeArtimis
Tim Diggles
Dave Kent
Ann Lambie
Rosie Lugosi
Cathy Nicles
Candra McKenzie
Steve Oakley
Steve Parks
Nick Pollard
Pat Smart